Outlines for Evangelistic Preaching

Outlines for Evangelistic Preaching

C. W. Keiningham

PULPIT LIBRARY

BAKER BOOK HOUSE Grand Rapids, Michigan 49506

PHOTOLITHOPRINTED BY CUSHING–MALLOY, INC.
ANN ARBOR, MICHIGAN, UNITED STATES OF AMERICA

Contents

Outlines for Evangelistic Preaching

1

Cure for Sin

Romans 6:23

1. Cancer is not the number one killer; sin is
   a. Cancer affects some; sin affects all
   b. Cancer kills the body; sin kills the soul—Matt. 10:28
2. Rejoice! A cure for sin has been found

I. Religion Is Not the Cure

A. Religion is designed by man for man. Every culture and person has a religion whether it be astrology, or materialism, or something else
B. Religion does not rid us of sin
   1. Cain's didn't—Gen. 4:1–7
   2. Cornelius—Acts 10

II. Ignoring Sin Is Not the Cure

A. No issue has ever been settled this way
   1. We can whistle for comfort in a dark cemetery, but the cemetery is still there
   2. Changing the subject doesn't eliminate the subject
B. This issue cannot be ignored
   1. Sin is the Loc Ness monster of the soul; we think the issue of sin is gone, but it reappears
   2. God doesn't want it to go away. He sends his Holy Spirit to convict us
   3. God wants sin faced and settled

III. God Offers the Cure to Everyone

A. God's cure is without cost—Rom. 6:23b
B. God's cure is offered to all—Rev. 22:17
C. God's cure has been found successful by millions
D. God's cure is simple—1 Peter 1:18, 19; 1 John 1:7

WS
11-25-84
MA/MZ

2

What Jesus Wants for You

1. What Jesus wants for you He has obtained
2. What Jesus wants for you, you cannot provide
3. What Jesus wants for you is had by abiding—John 15:4

I. The First Thing Jesus Wants for You—John 10:10
   A. Life—the basic need of every person
   1. The Bible says we are spiritually dead—Eph. 2:1. As a diver may die if his air hose is cut, so will we perish without our lifeline to God
   2. Abundant life speaks of the quality of life (cf. Eph. 1:3)

II. Another Thing Jesus Wants for You—John 15:11
   A. Joy in the fullest measure
   1. *Joy* means exhilaration of spirit, gladness
   2. Jesus never wants you to be "down in the dumps"
   B. Where does joy come from?
   1. Jesus called it "my joy"
   2. Joy doesn't depend on life's circumstances
   3. Joy depends on your relationship to Jesus
   C. Jesus wants your joy to be complete—John 16:24

III. A Third Thing Jesus Wants for You—John 16:33
   A. Peace is the great desire of everyone
   1. Some say peace is absence of conflict
   2. Jesus said we will have tribulation
   3. Peace is rest in the midst of conflict
   B. Peace is a gift from Jesus—John 14:27

IV. The Final Thing Jesus Wants for You—John 17:26
   A. Special love like the Father's for His Son—John 3:35
   B. Love shed abroad in our hearts—Rom. 5:5b
   C. All these gifts are received when Jesus is received

The Advocate

1 John 2:1

I. The Need for an Advocate
A. All must stand before God's Supreme Court
   1. We are accused of violating laws—Rom. 3:23
   2. We are accused by a formidable list of witnesses
      a. The Word of God is inerrant—2 Tim. 3:16
      b. The Holy Spirit is reproving—John 16:8
      c. Satan is vehement in accusation—Rev. 12:10
      d. Our own hearts condemn us—1 John 3:20
B. All need a divine advocate (lawyer)
   1. Someone to be on our side and plead
   2. Testimony of family and friends is irrelevant
C. Who will take our case?

II. The Name of an Advocate
A. A resume of our Advocate
   1. He has never lost a case
   2. He is the only One to win a case in this court
B. Who is our Advocate?
   1. "Jesus Christ the righteous"—1 John 2:1, 2
   2. Cases He has won: adultery, thievery, prostitution, etc.

III. The Nature of this Advocate's Defense
A. Propitiation is a peace offering (atonement)—1 John 2:2
   1. Jesus Himself paid for our sins
   2. Scars and blood are His testimony
B. Jesus must be brought into our case in much the same way as any lawyer
   1. We must invite Him to take our case—Rom. 10:13
   2. He stands at the door waiting—Rev. 3:20

4

How Shall We Escape?

Hebrews 2:1–4

I. **The Worth of Salvation**
   A. Prophets inquired of it—1 Peter 1:10, 11
   B. Angels desired to look into it—1 Peter 1:12
   C. Some angels risked damnation to gain like benefits—Isa. 14:12–15
   D. Salvation is entrusted only to the Son—Heb. 2:3
      1. Came to declare it
      2. Came to procure it

II. **The Reality of Salvation**
   A. The Lord Jesus confirmed it—Luke 19:10; John 3:16
   B. The disciples confirmed it—1 John 1:1
   C. The Father Himself confirmed it
      1. By the working of the Holy Ghost—Acts 10:44
      2. He confirms it in the same way today
         a. The government seal marks official documents
         b. The seal of the Holy Spirit marks God's Children—Eph. 1:13

III. **The Result of Neglect**
   A. Neglect always has dire results
      1. Farmer who neglects his harvest
      2. Merchant who neglects his business
   B. The Bible is full of examples
      1. Farmer with full barns—Luke 12:16–21
      2. Rich man and Lazarus—Luke 16:19–31
      3. Familiar patterns in all cases
         a. Preoccupation with worldly cares
         b. Neglect of soul's salvation
   C. We ought to give more earnest heed

5

His Name Is Wonderful

Isaiah 9:6

I. Wonderful in His Teaching
   A. Wonderful in its simplicity—Isa. 35:8
   B. Wonderful in its profundity
   C. Wonderful in its perpetuity—Matt. 24:35
   D. Wonderful in its mystery—Matt. 10:39; John 11:25

II. Wonderful in His Life
   A. Wonderful in its purity—2 Cor. 5:21
   B. Wonderful in its purpose—John 12:27
   C. Wonderful in its simplicity—Matt. 8:18–20
   D. Wonderful in its continuity—Heb. 7:25

III. Wonderful in His Person
   A. In Him dwells the fulness of the Godhead—Col. 2:9
   B. In Him there is life—John 1:4
   C. In Him there is sustenance—John 6:51
   D. In Him there is magnetism—John 12:32

IV. Wonderful in His Power
   A. Wonderful in the extent of it—Matt. 28:18
   B. Wonderful in its power to save—Heb. 7:25
   C. Wonderful in its power to keep—1 Peter 1:5
   D. Wonderful in its power to change lives—John 3:2
      1. Proof of Jesus' power is changed lives
      2. Jesus still has power to change lives
   E. Do you know this wonderful Savior?

6

Troubled at the Thought of God

Psalm 77:3

What about God troubles people?

I. The Righteousness of God
    A. The righteousness of God revealed
        1. Righteous in all things—Ps. 145:17
        2. Righteous for all time—Ps. 111:3
        3. Cry of heavenly creatures—Isa. 6:3
    B. The sinfulness of man revealed
        1. TV commercial with comparison of washed clothes
        2. Francois Maurice said, "No man can look at himself except down on his knees in the sight of God"
        3. Isaiah saw himself—Isa. 6:5

II. The Judgment of God
    A. Sin wouldn't trouble if there was no judgment
        1. Everyone shall give account—Rom. 14:12
        2. "Whatsoever a man soweth. . . ."—Gal. 6:7
    B. The certainty of it troubles—Heb. 9:27
    C. The righteousness of it troubles—Rom. 1:20
    D. The severity of it troubles—Ps. 90:7

III. The Rejected Love of God
    A. The love of God extended
        1. "God's love" is often a meaningless term
        2. A man dying and leaving a million dollars to someone is meaningless unless that someone is you
        3. God's love is extended to *you*
    B. The love of God can be accepted
        1. Extended through Jesus
        2. Accepted through Jesus

People Who Receive

John 4:46–54

I. The Man Heard

A. The importance of hearing
  1. Faith comes by hearing—Rom. 10:17
     a. Bartimaeus heard—Mark 10:47
     b. Andrew heard—John 1:40
     c. Philip heard—John 1:43
  2. People must hear about Jesus
B. The importance of telling
  1. Angel's word to Cornelius—Acts 10:6
  2. Jesus' word to the demoniac—Mark 5:19
  3. Good news is no news if it isn't told
C. The importance of what one hears
  1. The man heard that Jesus had come—John 4:47
  2. The hope of sinners is that Jesus has come—John 12:27

II. The Man Took Action

A. The importance of acting
  1. Hearing alone is not enough—Rom. 10:9, 10
  2. Lydia heard and "attended unto"—Acts 16:14
  3. Parable of the Great Supper—Luke 14:16–24
B. The danger of delay
  1. Danger of missed opportunity—Matt. 25:1–13
  2. Man's only contact with Jesus
  3. Sinners who delay are in great danger
C. The type of action needed
  1. The man invited Jesus into his home—John 4:47b
  2. The sinner must invite Jesus into his or her heart (cf. Matt. 7:7, 8 on the necessity of asking)

III. The Man Received

8

Paul's Teaching on Salvation

Ephesians 2:1

I. **The Need for Salvation:—People Are Dead in Sin**
   A. Dead and nearly dead are not the same
      1. Saved people can be nearly spiritually dead—Rev. 3:1, 2
      2. Unsaved people are said to be dead in sin
   B. Ways the unsaved are like the dead
      1. Unable to perceive things
         a. The senses of a dead person are inactive
         b. Natural man—1 Cor. 2:14
      2. Unable to appreciate things
         a. Child who pushes spinach aside
         b. Preaching of the cross—1 Cor. 1:18
   C. Valley of dry bones—Ezek. 37

II. **The Nature of Salvation—Quickening**
   A. "Quicken" means make alive
      1. It is a resurrection experience—Rom. 6:4, 5
      2. Made alive to God—Rom. 6:11
      3. Made alive to righteousness—Rom. 6:13b
   B. All need quickening for all have sinned—Rom. 3:23

III. **The Nominee for Salvation—You**
   A. We have many great discoveries in life
   B. The greatest discovery is that salvation is for you
      1. *You* are the object of God's love
      2. *You* are the target of God's effort

IV. **The Name in Which There Is Salvation—Jesus**
   A. Salvation is of the Lord—Ps. 3:8; Jonah 2:9
   B. Salvation is through Jesus—Acts 4:12; 10:43
   C. A man in Germany who was working on a church fell, landed on a grazing lamb, and lived. He later carved a figure of a lamb over the church door

9

Redemption

1. Three Greek words are translated to "redeem"
   a. One means to buy a slave at the market
   b. One means to bring a slave out of the market
   c. One means to set a slave free after buying him
2. Our redemption includes all three meanings

I. Humans Have a Basic Need for Redemption
A. Sin is the cause of this need
   1. Sin holds people in bondage—Rom. 6:16
   2. Sin causes misery
B. Sin is a product of our own doing
   1. We planted the bed of thorns we lie on
   2. We kindle the fire we burn in
   3. We dig the hole we fall into—Ps. 7:15

II. There Is One Who Can Redeem Us
A. Elohim is God's creative name
B. Jehovah is His redemptive, or covenant name
   1. Jehovah sent His son Jesus to redeem us
   2. Jesus was the price Jehovah paid

III. The Way Redemption Is Accomplished
A. Redemption is accomplished by the Savior's death. The Hebrew word for "blood" has the same root as "bless"
B. Redemption is appropriated by faith—Eph. 2:8

IV. There Is a Definite Purpose in Redemption
A. The primary purpose is to save people
   1. Redemption through the blood is *of* God
   2. Redemption through the blood is *to* God
B. The higher purpose—Rev. 5:9

10

Knowing God

John 1:1–5, 12–14, 18

I. We Can Know What God Is Like
    A. People have wondered what God is like
        1. Some see God as a tyrant beating the earth
        2. Some see God as a sentimental Casper Milquetoast
        3. A child drawing a picture of God was told that no one knows what God looks like. He said, "They will when I get through."
    B. Man's ideas are wrong. No man has seen God—John 1:18
    C. The Bible is a revelation of God
        1. Revelation is in the person of Jesus—John 1:18
        2. Men scoff at this idea—Rom. 1:23–25
        3. Only through Jesus can people know God
            a. Know what God is like—John 10:30
            b. Know God in salvation—John 14:7

II. What God Is Like
    A. Two words that describe God—"grace" and "truth"
    B. God is grace—love unmerited
        1. God loves us and is willing to receive us
        2. No sin is beyond His forgiveness
    C. God is truth—all reality
        1. The Bureau of Standards sets the standards of measurement
        2. God is the standard for truth and morality. Thus man cannot sin unnoticed

III. To Know God Is to Demand Decision
    A. God's presence is revealing—Isa. 6:1–5
    B. God's presence is redeeming—Isa. 6:6–7
    C. Salvation is possible through Jesus—John 1:12

11
The Coming of the Lord

2 Thessalonians 2:1–12

I. The Second Coming—What Is It?
A. We think of Jesus coming in the clouds
  1. Angel's words at Ascension—Acts 1:9–11
  2. He actually doesn't come to earth—1 Thess. 4:13–18
B. We see a later event (Jesus' coming to earth) in the text
  1. Spoken of in Matt. 25:31–32
  2. There are many events between these two comings

II. When Will It Be?
A. Some claim it has already happened
  1. Refuted by Rev. 1:7
  2. Some believed this in Paul's day—2 Thess. 2:2
B. Bible tells us exactly when Jesus' coming will be
  1. After final rebellion and falling away—2 Thess. 2:3
    a. Church attendance may be at an all-time high
    b. Abandon faith not church—1 Tim. 4:1
    c. Abandon Word of God—1 Tim. 4:3–5
    d. Divisions in the church—Jude 18, 19
    e. Description of troublemakers—2 Tim. 3:1-5
  2. After the Wicked One appears—2 Thess. 2:3
    a. He has many names: Man of Sin, Man of Lawlessness
    b. He is a beast rising out of the nations—Rev. 13:1ff.
    c. He will come in the power of Satan—2 Thess. 2:9
    d. He will perform wonders and deceive people—2 Thess. 2:9, 10a

III. What Does It Mean?
A. Hard to be saved then—2 Thess. 2:10, 11
B. End of opportunity
C. Judgment of the lost
D. Now is time to act

12

The Man God Called a Fool

Luke 12:16–20

Reasons the Lord called the man a fool:

I. He Thought More of His Body than His Soul
A. He made no provision for his eternal part
B. Many today follow the same course
   1. Body is dust; soul is eternal
   2. People travel miles for bodily healing

II. He Ignored God in His Life
A. He referred to "*my* fruits," "my goods," etc.
   1. He never acknowledged God as his partner
   2. He could easily have lost all as Job did
B. Riches can be a great blessing
   1. Wealthy people have a great opportunity to bless others
   2. Inordinate love of riches is evil
C. Danger is present when God is absent
D. Something not taken into account—v. 20 ("But God said")

III. He Failed to Include Others in His Plan
A. Old question: "Am I my brother's keeper?"
B. TV spot: "Parents, do you know where your children are?"
C. We have responsibility to others

IV. He Thought He Had a Lease on Life
A. He expected to live "many years." He was prepared to live but not to die
B. Many have this attitude today

13

The Lord's Purpose

Isaiah 53:10–12

I. **The Pleasure of the Lord—Isa. 53:10**
   A. Man's salvation is God's pleasure—2 Peter 3:9
   B. Man's redemption is God's personal concern
      1. If men perish, it is their own doing
         a. They go against the wish of God
         b. They climb over obstacles placed by God
      2. God is doing all He can to save men

II. **The Method of the Lord—Isa. 53:10–12**
   A. The salvation of people is possible. Reconciliation has been accomplished—Isa. 53:10–12
   B. Salvation for you is possible
      1. No matter how bad you have been
      2. No matter how long you have been bad
      3. Jesus saved thieves, prostitutes, evil rulers, etc.

III. **The Results of the Lord—Isa. 53:11–12**
   A. He brings people into fellowship with Himself—Isa. 53:11
      1. God's law condemns us—Gal. 3:10
      2. God's law carries the death penalty—Rom. 6:23
      3. God's law has been fulfilled—Isa. 53:11
   B. He brings people into the family of God—Isa. 53:12
      1. The Son (Jesus) is the heir of all things
         a. The word "portion" means inheritance—Luke 15:3–32
         b. The Son is the appointed heir—Heb. 1:2
      2. The saint is a joint-heir with Jesus. "If children, then heirs . . ."—Rom. 8:17

14

Three Parables
with One Lesson

Luke 15:1–24

1. Daniel Boone said, "I've never been lost in the woods but I've been confused for a week or two"
2. The wilderness is not the only place to get lost. Jesus told three stories about lostness

I. There Are Three Aspects of Being Lost
A. Being careless like the sheep, "All we like sheep . . ."—Isa. 53:6
B. Being helpless like the coin
   1. Coin's nature cause of falling—gravity
   2. Man's nature cause of being lost—Eph. 2:3
C. Being willful like the son
   1. Man is accountable. He has a choice

II. There Are Three Consequences of Being Lost
A. The sheep were confused and aimless. Man cannot find his way into fellowship
B. The coin was unusable
C. The son was degraded

III. There Are Three Searches for the Lost
A. Search of compassion—like the shepherd. God cares—John 3:16
B. Search of possession—like the woman (cf. Ps. 8)
C. Search of love—like the father

IV. There Are Three Results of Recovering the Lost
A. The sheep were safe
B. The coin was available
C. The son was back in fellowship with his father

15

The Demoniac

Mark 5:1–15

The demoniac has many similarities to a lost person

I. The Similarities
   A. Both dwell in the place of death
      1. The demoniac lived in a graveyard
      2. A lost person dwells in a state of death
         a. The unsaved are dead in sin—Eph. 2:1
         b. The saved have passed from death to life—1 John 3:14
   B. Both are beyond help by man's means
      1. The demoniac was bound with chains but he broke loose
      2. Men deal with the sinful nature by means of penal programs, rehabilitation, education, psychiatry, etc.
   C. Both are responsible for their own pain
      1. The demoniac cut himself
      2. To say that God sends people to hell is like blaming a would-be rescuer for the death of a drowning victim who refuses to be saved
   D. Both know who Jesus is
      1. The demoniac identified and worshiped Jesus
      2. A lost person is the only one of all God's creatures who does not bow to Jesus
   E. Both are troubled when confronted by Jesus

II. The Answer
   A. Jesus is the answer in both cases
   B. Jesus brings radical change—Mark 5:15; 2 Cor. 5:17

16

Repentance

I. The Doctrine of Repentance
   A. The Greek word means "change one's mind"
   1. Repentance is not just emotional feelings. One can shed tears and not repent—Heb. 12:16–17
   2. Repentance is not doing acts of penance
   B. The Hebrew word means "turn," "return," or "turn back"
   1. The Greek word denotes an inner decision
   2. The Hebrew word denotes an outward action
   3. Both can be seen in the prodigal son—Luke 15:11–32

II. The Importance of Repentance
   A. It is the first step toward salvation
   1. The unsaved are moving away from God
   2. The first step is to decide to change
   3. The next step is to turn back (action)
   B. It is the first response to the gospel that is demanded
   1. The gospel call is "repent and believe"—Acts 20:20–21
   2. Repentance precedes remission—Luke 24:46–47
   C. It is a direct command from God—Acts 17:30

III. The Nature of Repentance
   A. It is turning from dead works—Heb. 6:1
   1. The way of sin is the way of death
   2. The way of the world is the way of death
   3. The way of religion is the way of death
   B. It is turning to God's way—Acts 20:21

17

Salvation of Faith

Ephesians 2:8–10; Hebrews 11:6

1. Notice three things about salvation
    a. It is by grace—unmerited
    b. It is a gift—unearnable
    c. It is through faith
2. The issue of faith raises three questions to be answered

I. What Are We to Have Faith in?
   A. Abraham was justified by faith—Rom. 4:3. His faith was in God's Word
   B. Our faith is to be in the gospel—Rom. 1:16. Christ came, lived, died, arose, ascended, will return
   C. God's Word gives us clear directions for being saved—1 Cor. 5:1–4

II. What Is Meant by Faith in the Gospel?
   A. We hear various appeals made in churches—Believe on Christ, accept Jesus, open your heart, etc.
   B. All are calling for a response to the gospel
      1. Faith is not intellectual approval
      2. Faith is an active response to the gospel

III. How Does Salvation Come Through Faith?
   A. It does not come unsought
      1. Even food and drink don't come unsought
      2. Salvation must be received by faith
   B. It is emphasized in the Scriptures
      1. One must believe the facts of the gospel—John 3:16; Rom. 3:23
      2. One must claim God's provision by faith

18

The World's Greatest Gambler

Who is the greatest gambler in the world?
1. It isn't the casino gambler who bets all his possessions
2. It isn't the acrobat who walks the high wire without a net below
3. It is the sinner who puts off being saved (cf. Acts 24:24, 25)

I. He Had Heard the Message—Acts 24:24
   A. Paul pointed out the need—Rom. 3:23; 6:23
   B. Paul pointed out the hope (cf. John 3:16; 1 Tim. 1:15)
   C. Now you have heard the message

II. He Elected to Put Off Salvation—Acts 24:25
   A. Satan was at work—2 Cor. 4:3, 4
   B. Satan uses the same strategy today—1 Peter 5:8

III. To Put Off Salvation Is the Greatest Gamble
   A. Because your heart may harden
      1. More young than old get saved
      2. Truth rejected has a hardening effect
   B. Because you may never have another chance
   C. Because circumstances may never be as good—example of man delaying and woman marrying another
   D. Because you may die—no guarantee of life
   E. Because Jesus may come—Matt. 24:42-44
   F. Would you dare gamble with such high stakes?

A Look at Life

Psalm 119:57–64

I. A Determined Look at Life

A. The psalmist thought on his ways—v. 59a

B. Things that cause one to think
1. Tragedy—truck driver saved after wreck
2. Set-backs—man turned to God during bankruptcy
3. Dissatisfaction with life as it is
4. Desire to know life aright—psalmist

C. Things one perceives when he thinks
1. Futility—Eccles. 2:11
2. Sinfulness—Isa. 6
3. Potential—v. 61
4. Hope—v. 58

II. A Life-changing Decision

A. He made a definite decision
1. He turned his feet—v. 59
2. He intreated God's favor—v. 58a
3. He committed himself to God's way—v. 57
4. He put complete trust in God's Word—v. 58b
5. He aligned with God's faithful—v. 63

B. He was urgent—v. 60

C. A changed life requires decisions
1. Change of mind—repentance
2. Call upon the Lord—Rom. 10:13
3. Commitment of life to Christ—2 Tim. 1:12

III. A Personal Benefit

A. Psalm 51 was written out of the agony of sin

B. This psalm is written out of the joy of reconciliation

C. The joy of being saved is cause for singing

20

Regenerating Grace

1 Peter 5:10–14

I. The Means of Salvation
  A. Salvation understood
  1. It is a continuous process—1 Cor. 1:18
  2. It is a state of being—Gal. 1:l5–16
  3. It is a state of forgiveness—Eph. 1:7
  4. It is a state of justification—Titus 3:7
  5. It is a state of preservation—1 Cor. 1:8, 9
  6. It is a state of enabling—Eph. 3:7
  B. Salvation affected
  1. It is by grace—Eph. 2:8
    a. Grace begins—Titus 2:11
    b. Grace continues—Rom. 5:21
    c. Grace completes—Eph. 2:7
  2. It is through faith—Eph. 2:8

II. The Aim of Salvation
  A. Perfect people in Christ—Eph. 4:13
  1. State of completion—Col. 2:10
  2. State of submission
  B. Positive position in Christ—Eph. 2:6
  1. "Stablish"—fix firmly as in anchoring in concrete
  2. Strengthen—brace to solidify
  3. Settle (cf. Matt. 7:24–27)

III. The Person of Salvation
  A. God has called us by Christ Jesus
  1. Grace is extended through Jesus
  2. There is no salvation apart from Jesus
  B. Outside of Christ—outside of grace; outside of forgiveness—
    outside of heaven
  C. Jesus received is salvation received—John 1:12

Tale of a Happy Man

Psalm 32

I. **The Story of a Happy Man**
  A. "Blessed" means happy
    1. People seek happiness in many places—wealth, fame, popularity, sin
    2. This man found true happiness
      a. He found it in a relationship with God
      b. He found it in gaining forgiveness of sin
  B. Two sources of this man's happiness
    1. It was from having done right
    2. It was a gift from God

II. **The Story of What Led to Happiness**
  A. The Lord had something to do with it
    1. God dealt with him about sin
    2. There must be brokenness before healing
  B. The man had something to do with it
    1. He acknowledged and confessed his sin
    2. He cast himself upon the mercy of God
  C. The same process must be followed today

III. **The Story Is a Plea to All Sinners**
  A. It is a plea to those who are stubborn
    1. Text—don't be as a horse or mule
    2. Three reasons we are stubborn
      a. Because we love sin
      b. Because we are disillusioned with others
      c. Because we have no confidence in ourselves
  B. He found God because God was available (cf. Isa. 55:6)

IV. **The Story Is a Plea to God's Children to Be Glad**

A Thorough Washing

Psalm 51:7–13

I. **We Need to be Washed in the Blood—Rev. 1:5; 7:14**
   A. Three reasons we need to be washed in Christ's blood
      1. We are all sinners—Rom. 3:23
      2. Sin makes us unclean—Isa. 6:5; Matt. 23:27
      3. Only Christ's blood can cleanse us—Heb. 9:13, 14, 22
   B. Three things about this washing
      1. It is a spiritual experience—John 3:7, 8
      2. It is done by the Spirit—1 Cor. 6:11
      3. It places us in the body of Christ—1 Cor. 12:13

II. **We Need to be Washed in Water**
   A. Three reasons we need to be washed in water
      1. It is commanded by our Lord—Matt. 28:18–20
      2. It is a sign of obedience
      3. It is a public confession—Matt. 10:32
   B. It is by immersion—"baptizo"
   C. It is administered by the church—Acts 2:41–47

III. **We Need to be Washed by the Word**
   A. We need daily cleansing from our walk in the world
   B. Typified by the brass laver of the Tabernacle in Old Testament
      1. In the Tabernacle the laver was before the Holy Place
      2. Washing hands and feet were a prerequisite to entering
      3. Water here is a figure of the Word—Ps. 119:9
      4. See John 15:3; Eph. 5:25, 26; 1 Peter 1:22
   C. Accomplished by prayer and confession—1 John 1:9

23

Lost and Found

Luke 15:8–10

I. What One Must Do to Be Lost
   A. Most people have their own ideas
      1. They judge lostness by human standards
      2. This can be an obstacle to being saved
   B. Notice how the coin got lost
      1. It did what was according to nature
      2. It gave in to the pull of gravity
   C. People are lost in much the same way
      1. Adam determined the nature for man
      2. By nature we are the children of wrath—Eph. 2:3
      3. There is no need to commit hideous crimes to be lost

II. How One Can Be Found and Saved
   A. People have many ideas about this too
   B. Notice how the coin was recovered
      1. The woman brought light into the situation
      2. The woman went to work sweeping
      3. The woman looked everywhere the coin might be
   C. People get saved in much the same way
      1. Light has been sent—John 1:6–9
      2. The work of the church is seeking the lost
         a. We win souls in proportion to our diligence
         b. We are to leave no stone unturned

III. What Happens When One Is Saved
   A. There is rejoicing in heaven—Luke 15:7
   B. Three reasons for such rejoicing
      1. Difficulty in providing salvation—John 3:16
      2. Difficulty in reaching people
      3. Value of a soul—Mark 8:36, 37

24

Religious but Lost

Romans 10:1, 2

1. To be religious but lost is man's most perilous condition
2. This condition was common in Bible times. Cornelius, Lydia, Nicodemus, and Paul are some examples
3. Many people are like them today

I. Characteristics of "Religious" People
A. They believe in the existence of God
1. True of most world religions
2. Devils believe—James 2:19
3. Jesus said "believe also in me"—John 14:1
B. They depend on God to a degree
1. Cornelius was praying—Acts 10:2
2. Lydia was at a prayer meeting—Acts 16:13–15
C. They may be loyal to an institution by supporting it with attendance and finances
D. They ascribe to certain high ideals
1. Rich young ruler—Luke 18
2. Some people assume they are Christians because they don't smoke, drink, or curse
E. They may have a sensitive conscience

II. Mark that Distinguishes a Christian
A. Has had an encounter with Jesus Christ
B. Has made certain decisions and commitments to Jesus
C. Has had a life-changing experience
D. Has the Holy Spirit dwelling within
1. The issue involves more than "I believe in God"
2. Salvation depends on trusting Jesus as Savior

The Compassionate Christ

Luke 10:33–35, 37; Acts 2:36

1. One-word description of Jesus—"compassionate"
2. Christians "ought . . . also to walk"—1 John 2:6

I. The Objects of His Compassion
   A. The multitudes
   1. Stated five times in the New Testament
   2. In Matthew 9:36 they were scattered and distressed
   3. Masses are the same today—Isa. 53:6
   4. Christians should be compassionate
   B. The individuals
   1. Parable of the Lost Sheep—Luke 15:4–6
      a. Only one was absent; we would rejoice
      b. The shepherd felt personally responsible for that one
   2. We should feel more concern for people
      a. No one should be beyond our compassion
      b. No one should be given up on

II. The Manifestation of His Compassion
   A. In His feelings for others
   1. Never too busy to sympathize—John 11:33–36
   2. Never too busy to care—Matt. 20:30–34
   3. We should never be so busy—Rom. 12:15
   B. In his actions toward others
   1. The Good Samaritan is epitomized in Jesus
   2. Christians should act out of compassion—James 2:14–18
   C. In His willingness to pardon sin
   1. Notorious woman—Luke 7:48–50
   2. Jesus is still willing to pardon—1 John 1:9

26

The Power to Become

John 1:6–13

1. People have many desires and aspirations
2. Desire alone is not enough
   a. Man cannot achieve some things on his own
   b. Man cannot change himself—Rom. 3:12
   c. Culture is not enough
   d. Education is not enough
3. Man's need is very great

I. The Power to Become
A. "Power" here means right or authority
   1. Salvation is of the Lord—Eph. 2:8; Titus 3:5
B. The meaning of being a Christian
   1. Coming into a new relationship with God—"sons"
   2. Enjoying that new relationship
      a. Enjoying a new consciousness of God
      b. Enjoying a new security in God
   3. Having a new relationship with the world—John 17:14

II. The Peril of Rejection
A. Rejecting Christ limits what a person can be
B. Rejecting Christ is rejecting the only hope—Col. 1:27
C. Rejecting Christ is a strange choice. Consider our need and helplessness—Acts 4:12

III. The Plan of God
A. To make us his spiritual sons, his heirs and joint-heirs with Christ
B. To make any one of us his spiritual sons
   1. ". . . let him that is athirst . . ."—Rev. 22:17
   2. "Whosoever" in John 3:16 means *you*

Jesus' Death on the Cross

John 19:17

1. Christianity rests on two great events
   a. The death of Jesus on the cross
   b. The resurrection of Jesus from death
2. Both have to do with our salvation—Rom. 4:25

I. Text Declares the Cost of Salvation
   A. Salvation is God's free gift to man—Eph. 2:8
      1. It cannot be earned or bought—Rom. 6:23b
   B. Salvation is not without cost
      1. The cost was fully borne by Jesus—John 3:16; Rom. 5:8
      2. The cost was suffering on the cross—2 Cor. 5:21

II. Text Declares the Motive Behind Salvation
   A. Why did Jesus die on the cross?
      1. The wayward son of a godly father asked: "Why do you help? Why don't you just let me rot in jail?"
         "Because you are my son and I love you," the father answered
      2. Simple reason—Rom. 5:6–8
   B. Love is expressed in many ways
      1. Pakistanis kiss each cheek, Eskimos rub noses, the Ainu tribes people in Japan bite
      2. No expression compares to the cross

III. Text Declares the Method of Salvation
   A. The prophet Isaiah was given a glimpse
      1. Substitutionary death—Isa. 53:4–6
      2. The just for the unjust—1 Peter 3:18
   B. The plan is simple yet profound
   C. The transaction is complete only when we accept it—John 1:12

28

Theology in a Nutshell

Isaiah 53:6

I. The Way of Man Decried
    A. The way of man is called "gone astray"
        1. Not just the way of some—Rom. 3:23
        2. Like cattle out of the pasture and on the highway
    B. The way of man is considered urgent
        1. He has left the only safe harbor
        2. He is in a hopeless position—Eph. 2:12
    C. The way of man is born from within—James 1:14. He is in search of greener pastures and greater freedom
    D. The way of man is helped from without
        1. Attractiveness of sin—Gen. 3:6
        2. Temptations of Satan—Gen. 3:5

II. The Work of the Lord Revealed
    A. The work of the Lord is personal and redemptive for man—Matt. 18:11
    B. The work of the Lord involves the whole Godhead

III. The Wonder of Jesus Proclaimed
    A. Jesus is the central figure in the universe
        1. Government on shoulders—Isa. 9:6, 7
        2. Salvation on shoulders—Rev. 13:8
    B. Jesus is the wonder of the universe
        1. The wonder of His condescension—Phil. 2:7
        2. The wonder of His life—Heb. 4:15
        3. The wonder of His death—John 10:15, 18; 1 Peter 3:18
        4. The wonder of His love
            a. That obtained salvation for all
            b. That offers salvation to all

29

Love

1 John 3:1, 2

I. The Origin of Love—The Father
A. He is the epitome of love—1 John 4:8
B. He is the example of love—1 John 3:16

II. The Object of Love—Us
A. Man was created to be the object
   1. Created in God's image
   2. Capable of reciprocating
B. God loves man in spite of sin—1 John 4:10

III. The Achievement of Love—We Are Called Sons
A. Man is dignified by God's love—Ps. 8:4–6
B. Man is adopted into God's family—Rom. 8:15
   1. The world may not acknowledge us as sons of God—John 15:19
   2. The way of life should distinguish us

IV. The Intention of Love—What We Shall Be
A. Love's intention is future. God's plan for man is that we be like him
B. The Lord's intention is certain
   1. Jesus is coming—"when he shall appear"
   2. Queen Victoria said, "Oh, I hope He comes during my lifetime because I should so love to lay my crown at His feet"
   3. We shall see Him as He is
      a. Not as He was—in grief and sorrow
      b. As He is—in power and glory
   4. Then our change will be complete
C. God's love must be received—John 13:20

30

Forgiveness Understood

Psalm 130:4

1. Forgiveness from God is the best news anyone ever received
2. Those who appreciate God's forgiveness most are those who need it most
   a. Bread is common to many but is precious to the starving
   b. Air is glorious to the suffocating

I. There Is Forgiveness with God

   A. God's forgiveness is wonderful because it is true
      1. News that is suspected false has no impact
      2. Things which attest to its truth
         a. Consistent with God's nature
            (1) There is mercy—Ps. 130:7
            (2) God delights in mercy, not power, etc.
         b. Has given the best pledge—John 3:16. If there is no forgiveness the Cross is unexplainable
   B. God's forgiveness is wonderful because it is in the present tense
      1. There is forgiveness *now*
      2. Today is the day; now is the time—2 Cor. 6:2
   C. God's forgiveness is wonderful because it is unlimited
      1. Not just for certain number or type of sins
      2. Not just for certain people

II. The Purpose of Forgiveness Is that God May Be Feared

   A. "Fear" means reverence and respect. Fear must come before worship or service
   B. How forgiveness causes men to fear God
      1. Gospel of forgiveness builds faith—Rom. 10:17
      2. Gospel of forgiveness leads to repentance—Rom. 2:4
   C. He truly fears who accepts forgiveness

How to Be Saved

Acts 20:20, 21

How can a person be saved?
1. No question is more important
2. No question is more beclouded by Satan

I. God's Word Teaches but One Plan
   A. Day of Atonement in the Old Testament
      1. The high priest offered a sin offering
      2. The blood typified the blood of Jesus—Heb. 10:1
      3. Faith in sacrifices was an entitlement
   B. Day of Atonement in the New Testament
      1. Jesus offered Himself—Heb. 7:27; 9:26; 10:10
      2. There is salvation in no other—Acts 4:12
      3. Every sinner since Adam has been saved by Christ's blood

II. God's Holiness Demands Repentance
   A. The preaching of repentance
      1. John the Baptist—Matt. 3:8
      2. Jesus—Matt. 4:17; Luke 13:3
   B. The practice of repentance
      1. Means change of mind or attitude
      2. Results in a change of direction
   C. The permanence of repentance
      1. Comes from Holy Ghost conviction—John 16:8, 9
      2. Can be seen in life's actions

III. God's Son Merits Our Faith
   A. We are saved by His death—1 Cor. 15:3
      1. On Passover night only the blood saved
      2. Without the shedding of Christ's blood we can't be saved—Heb. 9:22
   B. We are saved through faith not feelings

32

Why Jesus Came

Luke 19:1–10

1. History tells us that Jesus lived
2. The Bible tells us why Jesus lived

I. To Show Man God's Love

    A. To show the reality of God's love
1. Showed in sending His Son—1 John 4:10
2. Showed in character of the Son
3. Showed in the death of the Son—1 John 3:16

    B. To show the intensity of God's love, He made the ultimate sacrifice—John 15:13

    C. Such love demands a response
1. Even dogs respond to affection
2. Zacchaeus was overwhelmed by such love

II. To Save Man from Sin

    A. Apart from salvation Christ's coming cannot be understood

    B. Purpose of Christ's coming given—Luke 19:10
1. Glorious song of the angels
2. Wonderful word to the wayward
3. Precious promise to the perishing

    C. The plan was simple—1 Peter 3:18

    D. One must accept deliverance by faith
1. Many said "I can't" and perished
2. Many said "I won't" and perished
3. Many said "Someday" and perished
4. Zacchaeus said "Yes" and lived

III. To Point Men to New Life

    A. Life with a changed outlook—Zacchaeus

    B. Life of purpose and peace—John 14:27

The Message They Preached

Acts 13:38–41

I. The Message Dealt with Sin and Judgment
    A. Identified sin as man's chief problem
        1. People search for answers in life
        2. People first need to know the questions
            a. Sin is behind confusion and misery
            b. Man's own doing—Ps. 7:15
    B. Pictured man as out of step
        1. Out of step with the universe
        2. Out of step with God—Isa. 59:2
    C. Visualized the consequences of sin
        1. Judgment of God is certain
        2. Judgment must be faced by every person

II. The Message Dealt with Repentance and Faith
    A. Man must repent of sin
        1. Two most common misunderstandings
            a. God is impersonal and doesn't care
            b. God is love and will not punish
        2. Two most common truths in the Bible
            a. God has acted on man's behalf
            b. Man must repent or perish—Luke 13:3
    B. Man must receive Christ by faith—Acts 16:31
        1. Salvation is in the person of Jesus—1 John 5:15
        2. The person of Jesus must be received—John 1:12

III. The Message Dealt with Forgiveness and Life
    A. They preached forgiveness of sins
    B. "If we confess our sins . . ."—1 John 1:9
    C. John Wesley said, "Before I can preach grace, I must preach law and judgment"

34

The Call of God

1 Peter 2:6–12

I. It Is a Transforming Call
A. The call of God is for men to be changed. God's purpose—Rev. 21:5
B. Four areas of change suggested
1. Quality of person—1 Peter 2:9
2. Conduct of person—1 Peter 2:12
3. Emphasis of person—1 Peter 2:11
4. Purpose of person—1 Peter 2:12

II. It Is a Transcending Call
A. Call transcends all boundaries
B. Call crosses every obstacle
1. No sinner is beyond the call—Paul, Zacchaeus, etc.
2. No person is too low or high—Acts 26:29
3. No person is too far or near—Mark 12:34

III. It Is a Transposing Call
A. A nobody can become a somebody—1 Peter 2:10
1. "Somebodies" are hard to find—Matt. 7:14b
a. God is no respecter of persons. The world's somebodies are not necessarily great in God's eyes
b. Sophistication substituted for character
2. God proposes to make us all somebodies
a. No child of God was ever a nobody
b. Translated into His kingdom—Col. 1:13

IV. It Is a Transitional Call
A. A change in the state of the person—1 Peter 2:10
1. Those far off are made nigh—Eph. 2:13
2. They have passed from death to life—1 John 3:14
B. A change in the destiny of the person
C. A personal call to you

The Rich Young Ruler

Mark 10:17–22

I. What the Young Man Had
A. He had riches
   1. The goal of many has been realized
   2. Wealth can be hazardous to your life
      a. Rich farmer—Luke 12:16–21
      b. Prodigal son—Luke 15:11–32
B. He had rule (authority)
   1. A man with authority has great opportunity. For example, see Cornelius and household—Acts 10:24
C. He had religion
   1. A Christian is a new creature not a religious one
   2. A Christian gives Jesus the central place in his life—Phil. 2:5–11

II. What the Young Man Was Seeking
A. He was seeking approval
B. He was seeking eternal life
   1. Most believe in life after death
   2. Most don't know where to go for reliable information
   3. This young man turned to Jesus

III. What the Young Man Was Offered
A. He was offered a cross
   1. It doesn't cost to *become* a Christian
   2. Yet it does cost to *be* a Christian
B. He was offered Christ
   1. He might have accepted something else
   2. He was faced with self-denial for Christ
C. He was not willing and went away
D. Are you willing to deny self and accept Christ as Lord?

36

What Must I Do to Be Saved?

Acts 16:22b–30

The question "What must I do to be saved?" is of great interest and concern
1. Because it expresses man's basic inquiry
2. Because it addresses man's greatest need
3. Because it deals with human happiness

I. Man's Answers to the Question

A. Suppositions based on Scripture
   1. Be a good neighbor and get along—Rom. 12:17, 18
   2. Be honest in dealings and pay debts—Rom. 13:8
   3. Provide for needs of family—1 Tim. 5:8
   4. Live a clean, moral life—Rom. 13:13
   5. Mind own business; earn own living—1 Thess. 3:11
   6. Live by the Golden Rule—Luke 6:31

B. These do not set forth the way to be saved

C. These set forth conduct expected of the saved

II. God's Answer to the Question

A. Notice how different God's answers are from man's
   1. His ways are not man's ways—Isa. 55:8
   2. God has chosen what seems foolish—1 Cor. 1:27–31

B. God's answer: Believe on Jesus Christ
   1. First reaction: Surely more is required
   2. Man cannot do what is required
   c. God required everything of His Son
      a. Including His death on the cross
      b. Jesus paid it all
   4. Salvation is a gift from God
      a. Provided by death of Jesus
      b. Obtained by believing on Jesus

37

Mephibosheth

2 Samuel 9:1, 6–13

I. He Was Turned Away

    A. Unable to claim his inheritance. He was crippled by a fall—2 Sam. 4:4

    B. We are unable to claim our inheritance. We have been crippled by the Fall—Gen. 3:1–7

II. He Was Sought Out

    A. He became the object of David's love and concern

        1. David didn't owe him anything

        2. David did it for Jonathan's sake—2 Sam. 9:1

    B. We are objects of God's love and concern

        1. God doesn't owe us anything

        2. God does it for Jesus' sake

III. He Was Brought In

    A. He was brought into the king's presence—2 Sam. 9:6

        1. The king's ambassadors brought him in—2 Sam. 9:5

        2. The king's presence made him feel unworthy—2 Sam. 9:6, 8

        3. The king presented his proposition

    B. Sinners are brought into God's presence

        1. Christians are God's ambassadors—2 Cor. 5:20

        2. Only there do they see their true self

        3. God presents His proposition through Word and Spirit

IV. He Was Lifted Up (Exalted)

    A. His inheritance was restored; his dwelling place changed

    B. He became secure when he was protected by the king and kingdom

    C. The same happens to a sinner when he or she is saved

        1. Inheritance—1 Peter 1:4; Rev. 21:1

        2. Dwelling place—Eph. 2:6

        3. Security—1 Peter 1:5

38

The Two Ways

Matthew 7:13, 14

1. Life is made up of choices and decisions. There is always at least two options—Rom. 8:1–4; James 3:13–18
2. The same is true of salvation; there is a fork in the road

I. The Two Ways Are Easy to Understand
  A. One way is man's way
    1. This is living to please oneself
    2. This is the course of the world—Eph. 2:2, 3
    3. This is the way of destruction—Prov. 14:12
  B. The other way is God's way
    1. This is living to please God
      a. Way of faith—Heb. 11:6
      b. Way of obedience—Rom. 6:16
    2. This is God's course—the Bible way
    3. This is the way of life—John 10:28

II. The Two Ways Are Opposites
  A. The contrast in the area of peace
    1. God's way is called the way of peace—Luke 1:79
    2. The wicked know no peace—Isa. 48:22; Rom. 3:17
  B. The contrast in the area of righteousness
    1. God's way is called the way of righteousness—2 Peter 2:21
    2. Way of unrighteousness—2 Peter 2:15
    3. Paul makes a contrast—Rom. 6:13

III. The Two Ways Are Every Person's Option
  A. We have the privilege of choosing
    1. Adam and Eve—Gen. 3:17
    2. Moses—Heb. 11:24, 25; Joshua—Josh. 24:15
  B. Everyone of us must choose—1 John 5:12

The Sure Foundation

1 Corinthians 3:11

1. The life of a believer is like the construction of a building—
   1 Cor. 3:9, 10; Eph. 2:22; Jude 20
2. The most important part of a building is the foundation

I. Foundation Required for Life—1 Cor. 3:11

A. Jesus is the only sure foundation—Acts 4:12; 1 Peter 2:6
B. How life gets founded on the Rock
   1. Matthew 16:13–17 closely resembles the way
      a. Personally confronted by Jesus
      b. Granted a direct, personal revelation
      c. Made a personal acknowledgment of belief
      d. Made an open confession
C. Today one is saved in much the same way
   1. Be personally confronted by Jesus through the gospel
   2. Receive direct revelation, see need, and answer. Revelation comes by the Word and the Spirit
   3. Acknowledge belief—Acts 8:35–38
   4. Confess Christ openly—Rom. 10:10

II. Why Is Jesus the Required Foundation?

A. Because we need an atonement for sin
   1. All are sinners and condemned—Rom. 3:23; 6:23a
   2. Jesus is the only One who can provide
B. Because we need new life
   1. We don't need a cleaned-up old life
   2. Jesus is the only one who can provide new life
C. What foundation are you building on?

40

At Peace Within

Philippians 4:7; 1 Peter 5:10

1. Peace comes as a gift from God
2. Peace comes as a result of being settled
3. Paul's peace came from being settled

I. Settled About Sin
    A. About the existence of sin (reality)
    B. About the nature of sin
        1. Anything contrary to God's Word
        2. Anything contrary to God's will—James 4:17
        3. Anything contrary to God's Spirit—Acts 16:6
    C. About the universality of it—Rom. 3:23
    D. About the consequences of it—Rom. 6:23; James 1:15

II. Settled About Salvation
    A. About the power behind it
        1. Not will power—John 1:13
        2. Not power of achievement—Titus 3:5
        3. Power of God—1 Cor. 2:5
    B. About the person of it—2 Tim. 1:12
        1. Some look to the church, etc.
        2. Some look to personalities (Jim Jones)
    C. About the permanence of it—2 Tim. 1:12

III. Settled About Service
    A. About what to do—2 Cor. 5:18-20
    B. About who is to do it—Eph. 3:1; "I, Paul"
    C. About why we are to do it
        1. We are debtors—Rom. 1:14, 15
        2. Wrath of God revealed—Rom. 1:18
    D. About where we are to do it—Matt. 28:18-20

Purpose of the Law

Romans 7:16; 1 Timothy 1:8

I. To Show Us Our Sinful Condition
A. That all may have knowledge of sin—Rom. 3:19-20
B. That sin might appear as sin—Rom. 7:7–13
   1. How would I know that stealing is wrong?
   2. Those not exposed to the law would kill without feeling

II. To Show Us We Cannot Save Ourselves
A. Many try to make themselves acceptable
   1. Israel—Rom. 10:3
   2. Justifying self not possible—Rom. 3:20
B. Facts must be faced honestly. See Paul's honesty in Rom. 7:18–23

III. To Point Us to the Savior
A. The law is a schoolmaster—Gal. 3:22–24
   1. A schoolmaster was a senior slave in charge of education. He taught foundational education then escorted the student to a school where one more able and capable took over the teaching
   2. When the child was delivered the slave's job was completed
   3. The law gives us a fundamental look at what God expects
   4. The law then delivers us to Christ—Rom. 8:3, 4
B. Law is a reflection of man's character
   1. Not a lot of do's and don't's
   2. Reflects man as a thief, adulterer, etc.
   3. Mirror pointing out his need—James 1:22–25
C. Christ Jesus came to save sinners—1 Tim. 1:15

42

Why We Need Jesus

Matthew 9:12

I. We Need a Stand-in (to Pay for Us)
A. The Bible says we are all sinners, yet some good people doubt their need of Jesus
B. The Bible says that the wages of sin is death—Rev. 20:14
C. We need someone to pay for our sin—Heb. 2:9

II. We Need a Stand-up (to Plead for Us)
A. This is how people stay saved
B. We need a lawyer with air-tight defense
1. Jesus ascended and went to the Father
2. Jesus offered our defense and sat down—Heb. 10:12
3. Jesus is able to save—Heb. 7:25
C. No other religion provides this

III. We Need a Stand-by (to Perform for Us)
A. Two impossibilities in life
1. To live the Christian life in own power
2. To satisfy God's demands on our own—Isa. 64:6
B. We need help in both areas
1. Jesus promised us a Helper—John 16:7, 13
2. No religious leader but Jesus promises this

IV. We Need a Stand-over (to Prepare for Us)
A. When going on a trip, we make preparations
B. We need to make reservations in eternity
1. Jesus is our travel agent—John 14:2b, 3
2. Jesus promised to prepare and transport us
C. This is why *you* need Jesus

43

Where Will You Spend Eternity?

John 3:14–21; Revelation 20:11–15

I. Where Do You Hope to Spend Eternity?
A. Where do you "hope," not "expect," to spend eternity?
1. To hope is to desire; to expect is to anticipate
2. A student may hope to pass but doesn't necessarily expect to
B. What are the alternatives?
1. Human opinion presents many—oblivion, annihilation, reincarnation, etc.
2. The Bible presents only two
a. Heaven and hell—paradise and torment
b. Everyone will spend eternity someplace

II. How Do You Plan to Get There?
A. People disagree on trip routes. The purpose of a map is to guide
B. What route do you plan to take?
1. Sinners are on the route to hell now. See the wide gate, broad way in Matt. 7:13
2. Everyone has an opinion on how to get to heaven
3. The Bible way is the only way—Eph. 2:8–10. God has given us a map to guide us—Rom. 10:8–10

III. When Do You Plan to Prepare?
A. Minneapolis Tribune poll of 1978
1. Seven out of ten believed in hell but only one in twenty-five believed he deserved hell
B. What does the Bible say?
1. All are sinners in need—Rom. 3:23
2. All are worthy of hell—Rom. 6:23a

44

What It Means to Be Saved

I. It Means to Be Safe
    A. Sinners seldom realize their peril
        1. Being lost is not just being unchurched
        2. The wrath of God is involved—John 3:36
    B. The saved undergo a lot of changes—Rom. 8:1, new standing; Rev. 21, new place

II. It Means to Be Satisfied
    A. No lost person is satisfied completely
        1. Satan tries to deceive us into thinking we are
        2. God has placed an alarm clock inside us
    B. The saved have a new attitude toward life
        1. Circumstances still may not be perfect
        2. Life has new meaning and purpose

III. It Means to Be Settled
    A. The unsaved are not settled about where they stand
        1. They lean toward God sometimes, sometimes not
        2. They are unsettled on issues of right and wrong
        3. Double minded—James 1:8
    B. The saved are settled about where they stand

IV. It Means to Be Secure
    A. Secure means under control
        1. There is an opposing force in life
        2. God tries to tie us down—to anchor us
        3. Man is out of control and under control—Rom. 6:11–23
    B. God's one great blessing—John 1:12